A Guide to Butterflies

(In Your Stomach)

Written by Sophia Rose, Illustrated by Alyssa Pontz

A Guide to Butterflies (In Your Stomach)

© 2024 Sophia Rose

Illustrations by Alyssa Pontz

ISBN: 978-0-9890934-8-4

Published in the United States of America by Mayfair Press.

A Guide to Butterflies

(In Your Stomach)

There are all different types of butterflies...

Monarch butterflies.

And Peacock butterflies...

There are even Zebra Butterflies!

But what about the butterflies that live in your stomach?

Before a shot at the doctor's?

Or meeting a new friend?

The butterflies in your tummy can feel quite fluttery! Flying around, they can make you feel worried and scared.

Princess Talk-A-Lots is in 4th grade. Every time she comes to class, she gets really nervous to see new friends. The butterflies in her tummy build up and build up, so she talks and talks, until the butterflies are so high up in the sky

she can't see them anymore.

4

Rowdy Rabbit is in Princess Talk-A-Lots'
class, too. Every time he's called on, he
gets too scared to talk and
doesn't know what to do with
his body. So he fidgets, and
fiddles, and jumps as
high as the Princess's
butterflies go.

The other kids sometimes don't understand.

One day, Jamboree the Jellyfish comes up to them and asks, "Why are you talking so much? Why would you ever need to jump so high?"

Princess and the Rabbit feel sad when their classmates don't get it.

"It's our butterflies," the Princess explains.

"Your what?" Jamboree the Jellyfish asks.

"The fluttery feeling in our tummies that makes us feel scared," Rowdy Rabbit says.

"Oh," says Jamboree. "I get that sometimes, too! But only before really scary things, like a rollercoaster."

"Sometimes I feel like I'm about to ride a rollercoaster right before I come into class. My throat feels tight, my tummy hurts, my heart goes a few beats faster than normal," says Princess Talk-A-Lots.

"How do you make yourself feel better?" Jamboree the Jellyfish asks.

"I imagine a place I like in my head," says Rowdy Rabbit. "I imagine myself all alone in the big, green meadow next to my house. It's my favorite place to go when I'm nearby, but when I'm not, I can always go there in my imagination."

"I like to breathe in deep," says Princess Talk-A-Lots. "I pretend to smell my favorite scent and then I blow out a big birthday candle. That usually calms me down!"

The teacher walks up to the front of the room.

"Listen up please, class," he says. "Today, everyone will be doing a project about your favorite animal, with a partner or by yourself, and presenting it to the class on Friday."

"Uh-oh," says Princess. "What if my project isn't good enough... what if my animal is too silly... what if I get up to the front of the class and I forget everything!!!"

Rowdy began to jump and jump, "Oh no, oh no," he whispers.

"Princess and Rowdy," says Jamboree. "I think it's your butterflies. Because a school project doesn't seem so scary to me."

"How is it not scary?" Princess asks.

"There's so many animals!" says Rowdy. "How will I pick the perfect one?"

"Well, I like monkeys, so I'm going to pick a monkey for my project," says Jamboree. "What animals are you guys thinking of?"

The Princess explains, "I'm thinking of maybe doing a cow, or a chicken, or a lizard, or a cat, or a dog, or a duck, or a..."

"Woah!" Jamboree interrupts. "That's a lot of animals."

"I wasn't done listing them yet," says Princess Talk-A-Lots. "Wait, maybe I could write them all down in a list."

So Princess makes a list of all her favorite animals. She begins to cross off the ones that may be too silly, too complicated, or too basic. After she crosses every other animal off the list, the only one left is a butterfly.

"A butterfly is a great idea!" says Rowdy. "I wish I had thought of that."

"Rowdy, how about we work together?" Princess asks.

"Oh," says Rowdy. "But what if you don't like the work I do, or if I have a great idea but you disagree, or you decide you don't want to be my friend anymore after working so much with me??"

"Rowdy," says Jamboree. "Princess is your friend. She won't stop being your friend even if she disagrees with you."

"Really?" Rowdy asks.

"Really," Princess confirms. "What if I love your work, or if we come up with great ideas together, or we become super best friends because of this??"

"That would be cool! Let's be partners."
Rowdy jumps.

Princess, Rowdy, Jamboree, and all of their classmates work and work on their animal project. They research, make posters, and write all their favorite facts down in different colors.

Then, comes Friday. It's the day to present to the whole class. "Um," says Princess Talk-a-Lots. "I feel really nervous. People might not like our presentation, Rowdy. It could be really embarrassing."

Rowdy Rabbit fidgets with his body and jumps up and down. "Maybe," he says. "But we worked super hard on this. I like our presentation."

The teacher comes up to Rowdy and Princess. "Are you two alright?" he asks.

"We're okay," Princess says. "But I feel nervous with all of my classmates watching me. I'm scared they won't like our project and we worked so hard."

"That makes sense. Sometimes I get nervous when I'm up in front of the class, too," the teacher says. "When I feel overwhelmed, I like to name 5 things I can see, 4 things I can touch, 3 things I can hear, 2 things I can smell, and 1 thing I can taste. It helps me focus on myself and my senses when there's a lot going on around me."

"I'll try that!" Princess says.

"Right now I can see 5 classmates. And, I can touch the 4 different posters around me. I can hear the sound of you talking, Rowdy hopping, and my own voice. I can smell lunch in the cafeteria and the cleaning wipes. I can taste my breakfast this morning, which was waffles and syrup."

"That's right," says Rowdy. He takes one big breath in and blows out a big birthday candle in his imagination. "We can do this."

"Princess and Rowdy," says the teacher. "When you're ready, the class would love to hear your presentation!"

Princess Talk-A-Lots pulls out the book she and Rowdy made and says, "This book is called *A Guide to Butterflies!*"

Rowdy begins to read...

What Kind of Butterflies Do You Have?

This is a great activity to do with a therapist or trusted adult!

1. Get one big sheet of paper, big enough to draw your body on. You can even lie down and have the adult trace your outline.

2. Draw 3 different types of butterflies: a big butterfly, a medium butterfly, and a small butterfly.

3. Think about the things that make you worry. These can be things at home, at school, with friends, or anywhere else in your life.

4. Write or draw each worry on a butterfly. Make as many butterflies as you need. Put the really difficult worries in the large butterflies, the sort of difficult ones in the medium sized butterflies, and the least difficult in the smallest butterflies.

5. Place the butterflies on your body drawing. Put them where you feel the worry in your body.

6. Once you have all your butterflies written out, start with the small ones and move onto the bigger ones. Think about what you could do or who you could go to in your life to help you with these.

Based on the play therapy technique, "Butterflies in my Stomach", an engaging assessment activity from Liana Lowenstein.

Sophia Rose has been writing since she could pick up a pencil. Nicknamed "Princess Talk-a-Lots" in her 4th grade class, she knows what it's like to deal with nervous butterflies. When she's feeling overwhelmed, Sophia likes to pet her dog or play fetch with him.

Alyssa Pontz has always loved to draw. She likes to doodle silly and cute characters that make others smile. When she is stressed, she cuddles her dogs or reads a book she likes.